olive

101 COMFORT FOOD CLASSICS

1 3 5 7 9 10 8 6 4 2

Published in 2008 by BBC Books, an imprint of Ebury Publishing
A Random House Group company

The Random House Group Limited Reg. No. 954009

Addresses for companies within the Random House Group can be found at www.randomhouse.co.uk

A CIP catalogue record for this book is available from the British Library.

The Random House Group Limited supports The Forest Stewardship Council (FSC), the leading international forest certification organization. All our titles that are printed on Greenpeace approved FSC certified paper carry the FSC logo. Our paper procurement policy can be found at www.rbooks.co.uk/environment

To buy books by your favourite authors and register for offers visit www.rbooks.co.uk

Printed and bound by Firmengruppe APPL, aprinta druck,
Wemding, Germany
Colour origination by Dot Gradations Ltd, UK

Commissioning Editor: Lorna Russell Project Editor: Laura Higginson
Cover design: Kathryn Gammon Designer: Stéphanie Achar
Production: Lucy Harrison Picture Researcher: Gabby Harrington
ISBN: 978 1 846 07569 8

olive

101 COMFORT FOOD CLASSICS

Editor

Janine Ratcliffe

Contents

Introduction

Comfort food is the culinary equivalent of a hug, and at **olive** we think it should be accessible any time, whether you have half an hour to spend in the kitchen after work or an afternoon cooking at the weekend.

With that in mind this collection is a soothing mix of well-loved classics as well as speedy solutions for more instant gratification.

In *101 Comfort Food Classics* you'll find recipes to suit every mood, so if you want a simple sofa supper, a slow-cook sharing dish for friends or a gorgeously indulgent pud then this is where you'll find them.

The **olive** team has picked out deeply satisfying recipes like *Sausages and mash with quick onion gravy* (pictured opposite, see page 24 for the recipe) which are guaranteed to hit the spot.

As always, all the recipes have been thoroughly tested in the **olive** kitchen to make sure they taste fabulous and work for you first time.

Janine Ratcliffe

Janine Ratcliffe
Food Editor
olive magazine

Notes and Conversions

NOTES ON THE RECIPES

• Where possible, we use humanely reared meats, free-range chickens and eggs, and unrefined sugar.

• Eggs are large unless stated otherwise. Pregnant women, elderly people, babies and toddlers, and anyone who is unwell should avoid eating raw and partially cooked eggs.

APPROXIMATE WEIGHT CONVERSIONS

• All the recipes in this book are listed with metric measurements.

• Cup measurements, which are used by cooks in Australia and America, have not been listed here as they vary from ingredient to ingredient. Please use kitchen scales to measure dry/solid ingredients.

OVEN TEMPERATURES

gas	°C	fan °C	°F	description
¼	110	90	225	Very cool
½	120	100	250	Very cool
1	140	120	275	Cool or slow
2	150	130	300	Cool or slow
3	160	140	325	Warm
4	180	160	350	Moderate
5	190	170	375	Moderately hot
6	200	180	400	Fairly hot
7	220	200	425	Hot
8	230	210	450	Very hot
9	240	220	475	Very hot

SPOON MEASURES

Spoon measurements are level unless otherwise specified.

- 1 teaspoon (tsp) = 5ml
- 1 tablespoon (tsp) = 15ml
- 1 Australian tablespoon = 20ml (cooks in Australia should measure 3 teaspoons where 1 tablespoon is specified in a recipe)

APPROXIMATE LIQUID CONVERSIONS

metric	imperial	US
60ml	2fl oz	¼ cup
125ml	4fl oz	½ cup
175ml	6fl oz	¾ cup
225ml	8fl oz	1 cup
300ml	10fl oz/½ pint	1¼ cups
450ml	16fl oz	2 cups/1 pint
600ml	20fl oz/1 pint	2½ cups
1 litre	35fl oz/1¾ pints	1 quart

Please note that an Australian cup is 250ml, ¾ cup is 190ml, ½ cup is 125ml, ¼ cup is 60ml.

Prawn laksa

20 minutes

medium rice noodles 50g
laksa paste 2–3 tbsp
half-fat coconut milk 400ml can
chicken stock 500ml
cooked large prawns 150g, from a sustainable source
beansprouts a handful
cucumber ¼, seeded and cut into strips
coriander leaves 1 small bunch, to garnish

■ Put the noodles in a bowl, pour over boiling water and leave to soften, 5–7 minutes.

■ Heat a pan, add the laksa paste and a splash of coconut milk. Fry for 3–4 minutes, add the rest of the coconut milk and the stock, stir, and simmer for 2 minutes. Add the prawns and heat through. Stir in the beansprouts. Put the noodles in 2 bowls, ladle soup over, and top with cucumber and coriander.

Serves 2

Look for laksa paste in jars in Asian grocers or in the spice section of larger supermarkets. Thai red curry paste would also work here.

Indian salmon cakes

30 minutes

sweet potato 1 large, about 300g, peeled and cut into small chunks
Indian curry paste 1–2 tsp
boneless skinless red salmon 1 can, about 180g
fresh breadcrumbs a large handful (whiz a couple of slices of bread in a food processor)
coriander leaves 1 small bunch, chopped
natural yoghurt 4 tbsp
olive oil
young leaf spinach 100g, wilted, to serve

■ Boil the sweet potato for 5 minutes then rinse in cold water. Drain really well and mash with the curry paste. Flake the salmon. Add to the potatoes with the breadcrumbs and half the coriander, mix and form into 4 cakes. Chill for 10 minutes. Mix the yoghurt and rest of the coriander, and season.
■ Heat 1 tbsp olive oil in a large non-stick pan and fry the cakes for 3 minutes each side until golden and warmed through. Divide the wilted spinach between 2 plates. Sit 2 cakes per person on top and serve with the yoghurt. **Serves 2**

Make sure you drain the sweet potato really well as it can retain a lot of water.

Mustard pork with spinach

20 minutes

olive oil
pork tenderloin fillet about 300g, fat completely trimmed and sliced
wholegrain mustard ½ tbsp
chicken stock 100ml
half-fat crème fraîche 2 tbsp
lemon ½, juiced
parsley leaves 1 small bunch, chopped
spinach 200g

■ Heat a large non-stick frying pan until hot and add 1 tsp olive oil. Quickly brown the pork slices all over in batches and scoop out. Add the mustard and chicken stock, bring to a simmer then whisk in the crème fraîche. Return the pork to the pan and simmer for 4–5 minutes until just cooked through. Season and add the lemon juice and parsley.

■ Meanwhile steam the spinach, divide between 2 plates, top with the pork and sauce, and serve. **Serves 2**

You can use Dijon or English mustard instead of wholegrain in this recipe. If using English, 1 tsp will be enough.

Mushroom and brown basmati pilaff

30 minutes

garlic 2 cloves, crushed
onion 1 large, halved and sliced
chestnut mushrooms 250g, sliced
butter 25g
brown basmati rice 250g
vegetable stock 500ml, hot
cardamom pods 4, bruised
natural yoghurt 6 tbsp, to serve
fresh chives 1 small bunch, snipped, to serve

■ Fry the garlic, onion and mushrooms in the butter for 5 minutes. Add the rice, stock and cardamom, cover and simmer for 25 minutes or until the stock is absorbed and the rice is tender. Mix the yoghurt with chives to serve. **Serves 4**

Brown basmati rice gives you all the nutty flavour of ordinary brown rice but is more delicate and cooks a lot quicker.

Ratatouille with crisp garlic sourdough

30 MINUTES

onion 1 large, finely chopped
garlic 3 cloves, 2 crushed, 1 halved
olive oil
aubergine 1 large, diced
courgettes 2, diced
red pepper 1, diced
chopped tomatoes 400g can
cherry tomatoes 250g
basil leaves 1 small bunch, torn
sourdough bread 4 thin slices

■ Cook the onion and crushed garlic in 1 tbsp olive oil in a non-stick pan for 5 minutes. Add the aubergine and cook for 10 minutes. Add the courgettes and pepper, and cook for 2 minutes, then add the tomatoes and simmer for 15 minutes. Stir through the basil.

■ Toast the sourdough, rub with the garlic halves and drizzle with 1 tbsp olive oil. Serve with the ratatouille. **Serves 2**

You could also serve this with some cooked rice or pasta, for a heartier dish.

Parsee spiced eggs

20 minutes

butter 25g
spring onions 2, sliced
root ginger finely grated, ½ tsp
red chilli 1, finely chopped
garam masala ½ tsp
cherry tomatoes 10, seeded and roughly chopped
eggs 4, beaten and seasoned
coriander leaves a small handful, chopped
wholemeal toast 4 slices, to serve

■ Melt the butter in a non-stick pan. Cook the spring onions, ginger and chilli for a couple of minutes, add the garam masala and tomatoes, cook for another minute and scoop out. Softly scramble the eggs in the same pan until creamy. Stir through the tomato mix and coriander. Serve with the toast. **Serves 2**

If you don't want a curried flavour, just leave out the garam masala from this recipe.

Chicken, pea and pasta broth

15 minutes

chicken stock 750ml
tiny pasta shapes or **rice** 50g
chicken breast 1, skinless, cooked and shredded
frozen peas 50g, defrosted
flat-leaf parsley a small handful, chopped

■ Heat the chicken stock in a pan, add the pasta or rice and cook until just tender – about 8 minutes. Add the chicken and peas, and cook for a minute until heated through. Season then stir through the parsley and serve. **Serves 2**

If you can't find tiny pasta shapes, you might use some broken-up spaghetti.

Sausages and mash with quick onion gravy

25 minutes

potatoes 500g, peeled and cut into large chunks
pork sausages 6, look for free range
caramelized red onions 4–6 tbsp, from a jar (such as The English Provender Co.)
beef or **chicken stock** 150ml
butter for mash
milk for mash

■ Boil the potatoes until tender. Meanwhile, grill the sausages for 10–15 minutes. Put the onions and stock in a pan and bring to a simmer.
Mash the potatoes with a little butter and milk. Season and serve with the sausages and onion gravy. **Serves 2**

Caramelized red onions are a brilliant storecupboard short cut. Stir into sauces for extra richness or use to top pizzas.

Hot-smoked trout kedgeree

10 minutes

eggs 3
microwaveable basmati rice 250g pack
spring onions 2, sliced
red chilli 1, finely chopped
butter
curry powder 2 tsp
hot-smoked trout 150g pack, flaked
parsley 1 small bunch, roughly chopped
lemon wedges to serve

■ Drop the eggs into boiling water for 7 minutes. Drain under cold water and shell. Microwave the rice for 2 minutes.
■ Meanwhile, cook the spring onions and chilli in a small knob of butter in a non-stick pan. Add the curry powder and cook for a minute then add the rice and stir well. Toss through the trout until warmed. Stir in the parsley.
■ Divide between 2 dishes and top with halves of egg. Serve with lemon wedges to squeeze over. **Serves 2**

Packs of microwaveable rice are a good stand-by, but you could use the same amount of cooked and cooled basmati. Make sure that it is piping hot before serving.

Three bean, tomato and spinach stew

30 minutes

onion 1 large, finely chopped
garlic 1–2 cloves, crushed
olive oil
ground cumin 1 tbsp
chopped tomatoes 400g can
kidney beans 200g can, rinsed and drained
cannellini beans 200g can, rinsed and drained
green beans 100g, chopped
spinach 100g, washed and roughly chopped
crusty brown bread to serve

■ Cook the onion and garlic in a little olive oil until softened. Add the cumin and cook for a minute. Tip in the tomatoes, plus a cup of water and simmer for 10 minutes, until thickened. Add all the beans and cook for 5 minutes. Add the spinach and cook for another 5. Serve with crusty brown bread. **Serves 4**

This is also good served with buttered couscous.

Pappardelle with lemon and sage mushrooms

20 minutes

pappardelle 150g
chestnut mushrooms 250g, sliced
butter 25g
garlic 1 clove, crushed
sage leaves 1 handful, shredded
lemon 1, juiced

■ Cook the pasta according to the pack instructions.

■ Soften the mushrooms in the butter, add the garlic, cook for a few minutes then stir in the sage and lemon juice. Drain the pasta, reserving 1 tbsp of cooking liquid, then toss everything (including cooking liquid) together and season. **Serves 2**

Adding a little of the pasta cooking liquid emulsifies the sauce and gives you a silkier result.

Chick pea soup with shredded greens and chorizo

30 minutes

onion 1, chopped
garlic 2 cloves, chopped
olive oil
chickpeas 2 x 400g cans, drained
chicken stock 750ml
dried chilli flakes a pinch
spring greens, Savoy cabbage or **curly kale** 150g, shredded
chorizo 4 slices, shredded

■ Fry the onion and garlic in a little olive oil until softened. Add the chick peas, chicken stock and chilli. Cook for about 10 minutes then stir in the greens and cook for 3 minutes. Spoon into bowls and add the chorizo. **Serves 4**

Try to buy chorizo in a large piece rather than ready sliced. It will keep for ages in the fridge, and you can just slice it as you need it.

Butternut squash chilli with quinoa

30 minutes

onion 1 large, finely chopped
garlic 2 cloves, crushed
olive oil
mild chilli powder 1 tbsp (look for one containing added cumin, oregano and garlic)
butternut squash 1, about 1kg, peeled and cubed
quinoa 100g, soaked in cold water for 10 minutes
chopped tomatoes 2 x 400g cans
red kidney beans 400g can
coriander leaves 1 small bunch, chopped

■ Cook the onion and garlic in 1 tbsp olive oil until soft (about 7 minutes). Add the chilli powder, cook for a minute then add the squash, quinoa and tomatoes. Simmer for 10–15 minutes until the squash and quinoa are tender and the sauce has thickened. Add the beans and heat through. Stir in most of the coriander and serve in bowls, sprinkled with remaining coriander. **Serves 4**

Quinoa is a high-protein grain available from health-food shops and some supermarkets.

Chinese chicken noodle broth

10 minutes

chicken stock 600ml
soy sauce 2 tbsp
sesame oil 1 tbsp
fine egg thread noodles 50g
shiitake mushrooms 100g, halved
cooked chicken breast 2, skinless and shredded
young leaf spinach 50g
red chilli 1, seeded and shredded, to garnish

■ Heat the stock, soy sauce and sesame oil in a pan, and cook the noodles and mushrooms in the stock mix for 2 minutes. Add the chicken and spinach, and heat through for a few more minutes. Ladle the broth into bowls, scatter with chilli and serve. **Serves 2**

For a vegetarian soup, just add veg such as mangetout and sliced peppers instead of the chicken and use vegetable stock.

Polenta with mushroom and sage butter

30 minutes

instant polenta 100g
Parmesan 25g, freshly grated, plus extra shavings to serve (optional)
butter 100g
mixed mushrooms 2 handfuls, halved, quartered or sliced
sage leaves a few, shredded

■ Make up the polenta according to the pack instructions then beat in the cheese with half the butter and season really well. You want it quite soft and unctuous.
■ Melt the rest of the butter in a pan and cook the mushrooms until golden, add the sage and stir. Serve the polenta topped with the mushroom mix and some extra parmesan shavings, if you like. **Serves 2**

Instant polenta cooks in minutes and is much easier to use than regular.

Portobello mushroom melts

15 minutes

large portobello mushrooms 8
olive oil
pesto 2–3 tbsp, fresh or from a jar
mozzarella 1 ball
pine nuts 2 tbsp
ciabatta 8 slices

■ Put the mushrooms in a lightly oiled ovenproof dish and drizzle the pesto over. Tear the cheese into pieces and divide among the mushrooms. Sprinkle over the pine nuts and grill under a low heat for 8–10 minutes until the cheese is bubbling and melted.

■ Meanwhile, lightly toast the ciabatta. Serve a mushroom on each slice of toast.

Serves 4

Look for large, flat mushrooms, sometimes called field mushrooms.

Tomato, spinach and mascarpone gnocchi

20 minutes

ready-made gnocchi 500g pack
tomato pasta sauce 350g jar
spinach 100g, washed
mascarpone 250g carton
Parmesan or **Grana Padano** 50g

■ Cook the gnocchi according [illegible] instructions and drain. Meanw[illegible] the tomato sauce in an ovenpro[illegible] and add the spinach, stirring u[illegible]

■ Add the gnocchi, season an[illegible] blobs of mascarpone over. Sc[illegible] shavings of Parmesan or Grana Pad[illegible] and grill until bubbling and golden.

Serves 4

There are some really good-quality pasta sauces available. Look for one with few ingredients, made with olive oil.

Sausage and butternut squash pasta

30 minutes

onion ½, chopped
butternut squash 250g, peeled and cut into small cubes
sausages 4–6, skins removed and cut into chunks
olive oil
linguine 200g, cooked
parsley a small handful, chopped
basil leaves 1 small handful, chopped
chilli oil to serve (optional)

■ Fry the onion, butternut squash and sausage pieces together in a little olive oil for about 10 minutes or until cooked. Toss through the linguine along with the herbs and lots of seasoning. Serve with chilli oil, if you like. **Serves 2**

Choose good-quality sausages with lots of seasoning and high meat content.

Chilli-crusted steak with mustard mash

30 minutes

floury potatoes 500g, such as King Edward
fresh white breadcrumbs 50g
olive oil
dried chilli flakes 1 tsp
fresh chives and **parsley leaves** 1 tbsp of each
rump steak 2, about 200g each
butter for mash
milk for mash
wholegrain mustard 1½ tbsp, for mash

■ Boil the potatoes until tender, 15–20 minutes. Meanwhile, blend the breadcrumbs, 2 tbsp oil, chilli flakes and herbs in a food processor and season.
■ Heat a griddle pan (chargrill) to very hot. Season and lightly oil the steaks and griddle for 2 minutes each side for rare (3 for medium). Spoon the breadcrumb mix over the steaks and flash under the grill until golden brown.
■ Mash the potatoes with a little butter, milk and seasoning and stir through the mustard. Serve the steaks with the mustard mash. **Serves 2**

If you don't like too much heat, you could substitute a big pinch of paprika for the chilli.

Thai coconut chicken

20 minutes

Thai red curry paste 1–2 tbsp, depending on how hot you like it
half-fat coconut milk 400ml can
boneless skinless chicken breasts 2, cut into strips
green beans 100g
cherry tomatoes 100g
brown rice 100g, steamed, to serve

■ Stir fry the curry paste in a splash of the coconut milk until fragrant. Add the rest of the milk and bring to a simmer. Add the chicken and beans and simmer for 5 minutes. Add the tomatoes and simmer for another 3 minutes. Serve with brown rice. **Serves 2**

Curry pastes vary quite widely in strength so just add a little to begin with – you can always add more later.

Butternut squash lasagne

30 minutes

onion 1, finely sliced
oil for frying
butternut squash 500g, peeled and cut into small cubes
ground cinnamon a pinch
whole nutmeg for grating
milk 100ml
frozen leaf spinach 150g
fresh lasagne sheets 3
mozzarella 1 ball, about 125g

■ Fry the onion in a little oil until soft, add the butternut squash and fry until tender and slightly browned around the edges. Add the cinnamon, a grating of nutmeg and the milk and mash roughly. Heat the spinach with another grating of nutmeg.

■ Meanwhile, cook the lasagne sheets in boiling water for 3 minutes and drain. Put a sheet of lasagne in a small baking dish, add a layer of butternut squash and half the spinach. Season. Add another layer of lasagne and the rest of the butternut squash and spinach. Season and follow with a final layer of lasagne. Rip the mozzarella into pieces and scatter it over the final sheet, grill briefly until the mozzarella bubbles and browns.
Serves 2

You can use fresh spinach for this when in season. Just add to a hot pan with a little olive oil and stir until wilted.

Bacon and roasted tomato risotto

30 minutes

oil for frying
onion 1, finely chopped
garlic 1 clove, crushed
back bacon rashers 4, fat cut off, finely chopped
risotto rice: carnaroli or **arborio** 200g
chicken stock 1 litre
cherry tomatoes 12, take off the stalks, if you prefer

■ Heat a little oil in a wide pan and fry the onion gently for a few minutes until soft. Add the garlic and half of the bacon and fry everything together. Add the rice and stir well and then add the hotstock a couple of ladles at a time, stirring each lot in until it is completely absorbed and the risotto is creamy but still retains a little bite (you might not need to use all of the stock).

■ Meanwhile, heat another pan with a little oil and cook the remaining bacon with the tomatoes over a high heat until browned. Spoon over the risotto to serve.

Serves 2

The amount of stock you use in a risotto will depend on the absorbency of your rice. You might not need all of it, or you could need to add a little extra water at the end.

Prawn and harissa stew with couscous

20 minutes

couscous 100g
olive oil for frying
chicken stock 200ml
onion 1 small, sliced
garlic 2 cloves, crushed
ground cumin 1 tsp
chopped tomatoes 400g can
harissa 1–2 tsp
raw peeled prawns 150g
coriander leaves from 1 small bunch

■ Put the couscous in a bowl with 1 tsp olive oil and just enough boiling chicken stock to cover. Cover and leave to swell for 5 minutes.
■ Heat 1 tbsp oil in a pan, add the onion and garlic and fry for 1–2 minutes or until just tender. Add the cumin and fry for a minute, add the tomatoes and harissa and bubble everything together until it thickens slightly. Season well.
■ Stir in the prawns and cook for 3 minutes, then scatter the coriander over. Serve with the couscous. **Serves 2**

You can substitute sliced chicken breast for the prawns – just give it 5 more minutes' cooking.

Steak and onions with celeriac mash

30 minutes

celeriac 1 small, peeled and cut into chunks
milk
oil
sirloin steaks 2, thick cut
red onion 1, sliced
red wine 1 glass
brown sugar 1 tsp

■ Simmer the celeriac in water for about 15 minutes or until it is tender. Drain and mash with a little milk and lots of seasoning.

■ Put a little oil in a hot frying pan and add the steaks. Add the onion around the edges and cook for 2 minutes. Turn over the steaks and stir the onions around. After 2 minutes add the red wine and brown sugar, and bubble everything together to make a sauce. Season well and serve with the mash. **Serves 2**

If you want a super-smooth mash, whiz the celeriac and milk in a food processor.

Very quick chicken casserole

30 minutes

skinless chicken thigh fillets 4 large or 6 small
shallots 3, quartered
carrot 1, sliced
new potatoes or **salad potatoes** 8, skin left on and halved or quartered if large
chicken stock 500ml
frozen peas 1 cupful
tarragon leaves 1 small bunch, chopped

■ Put the chicken thighs, shallots, carrot, potatoes, some seasoning and the stock in a wide casserole and bring to a simmer. Cover and cook for 15 minutes, then add the peas and tarragon, and cook for a further 10 minutes or until the potato is tender and serve. **Serves 2**

You can stir a spoonful of crème fraîche into the sauce at the end, if you prefer a creamier sauce.

30-minute fish pie

30 minutes

filo pastry 2 sheets
butter 1 tbsp
flour 1 tbsp
milk 250ml
bay leaf 1
skinless white fish and/or **salmon fillets**, about 350g, cut into cubes
small cooked prawns 100g
parsley leaves a handful, chopped

■ Heat the oven to 180C/fan 160C/gas 4. Lay the filo sheets on top of each other on a baking sheet, and scrunch them up into a size that will fit the top of the pie dish you want to use. Bake for 8 minutes or until the filo has cooked and turned golden.

■ Meanwhile, melt the butter and stir in the flour, let it foam for a minute and then gradually whisk in the milk, and add the bay leaf. Bring to a simmer and cook for 2–3 minutes or until the mixture thickens. Fold in the fish, prawns and parsley, and cook gently for 5 minutes or until the fish has cooked through. Tip into a warmed pie dish and sit the filo on top. **Serves 2**

If you want to make a conventional fish pie, just top the filling with mash and bake for another 10–15 minutes in a hot oven.

Mozzarella in carrozza

20 minutes

white bread 8 slices
mozzarella 1 ball, sliced into 4
basil leaves 8 large
flour 2 tbsp, well seasoned
eggs 2, beaten with a splash of milk and seasoned
olive oil for frying
sea salt flakes to sprinkle

■ Use a cutter or large mug to cut circles (about 10cm) from the bread. Divide the cheese among 4 of the circles, adding a basil leaf on either side of the cheese. Season, then put the rest of the bread circles on top, pressing the edges together.

■ Put the flour on to a plate. Dust the sandwiches in the flour to coat lightly, then dip them in the egg completely to coat. Heat a large non-stick frying pan with 2 tbsp olive oil. Fry the sandwiches for about 3 minutes each side until crisp and golden. Sprinkle with sea salt flakes and serve. **Serves 2**

This classic Italian recipe translates as 'mozzarella in a carriage', the carriage being the bread that holds the cheese.

Scrambled egg, smoked trout and chive bagels

15 minutes

bagels 2, split
butter 25g
eggs 4
smoked trout 50g slices
fresh chives a few, snipped, to garnish

■ Toast the bagel halves. Melt the butter in a pan, then add the eggs and heat slowly, stirring until softly scrambled and creamy. Put 2 bagel halves on to each plate, drape over the smoked trout then pile up the scrambled egg. Scatter over the chives and serve. **Serves 2**

For a vegetarian version, leave out the trout and stir a handful of wilted spinach through the scrambled egg.

Warm chick pea and cumin flatbreads with yoghurt dip

10 minutes

olive oil for frying
cumin seeds 1 tsp, crushed
green chilli 1, finely chopped
chick peas 400g tin, drained and rinsed
cherry tomatoes 100g, quartered
lime ½, juiced
flatbreads 4

YOGHURT DIP
coriander leaves a small handful, chopped
natural yoghurt 150g

■ Heat 1 tbsp oil in a small frying pan and gently fry the cumin for a minute to release the flavour. Add the chilli, chick peas and tomatoes, and stir to coat in the cumin and oil. Cook for a couple of minutes and crush slightly, then add the lime juice.

■ To make the dip, stir the coriander through the yoghurt. Warm the flatbreads following the pack instructions. Divide the chick pea mix among the flatbreads and roll them up. Serve with the yoghurt dip. **Serves 2**

You could also use pitta breads or flour tortillas instead of flatbreads.

Bacon, pear and Roquefort muffins

20 minutes

streaky bacon rashers 4, cut into pieces
pear 1 ripe, cored and sliced
muffins 4, spilt and toasted
Roquefort cheese 100g, crumbled

■ Fry the bacon in a non-stick pan until just turning crisp then scoop out. Cook the pear slices for a couple of minutes in the same pan until lightly golden on both sides.

■ Divide the pears and bacon among the muffins. Sprinkle over the Roquefort cheese and grill until the cheese is golden and bubbling. Serve with salad.

Serves 2

Other blue cheeses like Stilton or Gorgonzola would also work for this.

Thai-style turkey burgers

30 minutes

minced turkey 400g
spring onions 4, finely chopped
root ginger grated, 1 tsp
red chilli 1, seeded and finely chopped
egg 1 yolk
coriander leaves 1 small bunch, chopped
sunflower oil 1 tbsp
ciabatta rolls 4
watercress a few sprigs
sweet chilli sauce to serve (optional)

■ Put the first 6 ingredients in a bowl, season and mix well. Form into 4 burgers. Heat the oil in a non-stick frying pan and fry the burgers for about 5 minutes on each side until golden and cooked through. Serve the burgers in rolls with some watercress and a little sweet chilli sauce, if you like. **Serves 4**

The easiest way to mix this is to use your hands to distribute the flavours properly.

Pepper, red onion and goat's cheese frittata

15 minutes

eggs 6
oil
red onion 1, halved and sliced
red pepper 1, chopped into 2cm pieces
goat's cheese 100g
paprika ½ tsp
parsley and/or **chives** 1 small handful, roughly chopped
salad to serve

■ Beat the eggs and season well. Heat 1 tbsp oil in a small non-stick frying pan and cook the onion and red pepper for 3–4 minutes to soften. Add the eggs and cook for 5–6 minutes until almost set.

■ Dot the goat's cheese over the eggs, then scatter the paprika and herbs over the top, and slide under a hot grill for 2–3 minutes until golden. Cut into wedges and serve with salad. **Serves 2**

You can serve this frittata hot or cold – it makes a great picnic food.

Welsh rarebit

30 minutes

mature Cheddar 250g
English mustard 1 tsp
egg yolk 1
Worcestershire sauce a couple of good dashes
Guinness 1–2 tbsp
sourdough or **other crusty bread** 8 slices

■ Put all the ingredients except the Guinness and bread in a small food processor and whiz, adding enough Guinness to make a paste. Toast the bread then thickly spread on the rarebit. Grill until golden and bubbling. **Serves 4**

You can also use this mix as a topping for grilled tomatoes or steak.

Corn, chive and prawn chowder

30 minutes

sweetcorn 2 cobs, kernels removed
spring onions 4, sliced
potato 1 large, peeled and diced
butter
light chicken stock 750ml
double cream 4 tbsp
North Atlantic peeled cooked prawns 150g
fresh chives 1 small bunch, snipped

■ Cook the corn, spring onions and potato gently in a knob of butter for 2 minutes. Add the stock and simmer for 8–10 minutes until the potato and corn are tender. Stir in the cream and prawns, season and simmer until the prawns are just heated through. Stir in the chives and serve. **Serves 4**

To remove the kernels from sweetcorn, stand the cob on its end and cut down with a sharp knife.

Baked goat's cheese with toasted brioche

20 minutes

antipasti marinated onions 6, halved
tomato chutney 2 heaped tsp
soft goat's cheese 100g
olive oil
brioche toasted, to serve

■ Put the onions in the bottom of 2 ramekins and add 1 tsp chutney to each. Add half of the goat's cheese to each and drizzle with olive oil. Grill under a medium heat for 8–10 minutes, or until the cheese is bubbling and browned. You need to give this a decent amount of time or the onions won't warm through. Serve with the brioche. **Serves 2**

If you can't find antipasti onions, use a spoonful of caramelized onions from a jar in the bottom of each ramekin.

Spiced sole goujons with lemon mayo

30 minutes

fresh breadcrumbs 100g
cayenne pepper ½ tsp
lemon sole 4 skinless fillets, cut into 1cm-thick long strips
plain flour 50g
eggs 2, beaten
lemon a squeeze of juice, to taste
mayonnaise 3 tbsp
salad leaves to serve

■ Mix the breadcrumbs with the cayenne pepper. Season the fish then coat a few pieces at a time in the flour, then the beaten egg and finally the breadcrumbs. Lightly oil a non-stick baking sheet. Spread the goujons out on the tray and grill for 2–3 minutes each side, until crisp, golden and cooked through.

■ Mix the lemon juice into the mayonnaise, season and serve with the goujons and some salad leaves. **Serves 2**

You can use any firm white fish to make these goujons.

Baked eggs with ham and tomato

20 minutes

olive oil
garlic 1 clove, chopped
chopped tomatoes 400g can
basil leaves a few, shredded
cooked ham 4 slices, roughly torn
eggs 2
crusty bread to serve

■ Heat the oven to 180C/fan 160C/gas 4. Heat a little oil in a pan, sizzle the garlic for a few seconds then add the tomatoes and simmer for 10 minutes until thickened. Stir in the basil.

■ Divide the sauce and ham between 2 individual baking dishes. Crack an egg on top and season. Bake for 12–14 minutes until just set. Serve with crusty bread.

Serves 2

Top these with some mature Cheddar for an extra-rich finish.

Chicken and Peppadew quesadillas

30 minutes

flour tortillas 8
cooked chicken breasts 2, sliced
Peppadew sweet peppers 150g, drained and roughly chopped
red onion ½, finely sliced
rocket a handful
Comté or **Gruyère cheese** 200g, freshly grated

■ Sprinkle 4 tortilla wraps evenly with all the ingredients. Top with the remaining tortillas. Heat a non-stick frying pan and cook each for 3–4 minutes until the cheese begins to melt and stick together, and the tortilla browns. Carefully flip over and brown the other side. Cut each quesadilla into 4 wedges and serve.
Serves 4

Peppadew are sweet and hot pickled peppers. Find them in jars in supermarkets.

Sweet chilli pork burgers

30 minutes

minced pork 400g
onion 1, grated
garlic 2 cloves, crushed
sweet chilli dipping sauce 2 tbsp
coriander leaves a small handful, chopped
fresh breadcrumbs 3 tbsp
egg yolk 1, beaten
sunflower oil
ciabatta rolls 4, halved and lightly toasted
tomatoes 2, sliced
red onion 1 small, sliced

■ Mix together the pork, onion, garlic, sweet chilli sauce, coriander, breadcrumbs and egg yolk in a bowl with your hands. Season and form into 4 burgers. Fry the burgers in 1 tbsp oil for 5–6 minutes each side over a medium heat, or until cooked through. Arrange each burger on a ciabatta base, top with sliced tomatoes, red onion, a little more sweet chilli sauce and the ciabatta top to serve. **Serves 4**

If you like a bit more heat, add a chopped red chilli to the burger mix.

Stir-fried spicy beef rice with greens

30 minutes

lean sirloin or **frying steak** about 250g, trimmed of all fat and cut into thin strips
sunflower oil
root ginger 1 thumb-sized piece, shredded
Chinese five-spice 2 tsp
spring greens 200g, shredded
soy sauce 1 tbsp
micro-waveable brown basmati 1 pack, heated according to pack instructions
spring onions 4, shredded
red chilli 1, shredded

■ Stir fry the beef in 1 tbsp oil until browned then add the ginger and fry for a minute. Add the five-spice, cook for another minute then add the greens with a splash of water and the soy, and stir fry until just tender. Add the rice and toss everything together. Serve in bowls topped with spring onions and chilli. **Serves 2**

You can use any greens in this – spinach, bok choi or broccoli would all work well.

Spring onion, Wensleydale and ham pastries

40 minutes + chilling

spring onions 4, shredded
Wensleydale cheese 100g, grated
cooked ham 100g thick cut, chopped
eggs 2, beaten
ready-rolled shortcrust pastry 1 sheet, cut into 4 rectangles

■ Heat the oven to 190C/fan 170C/gas 5. Mix together the onions, cheese, ham and ½ the egg. Season. Divide the mix among the pastry, putting it on one 1/2 of each rectangle. Fold each over to make a parcel and crimp together the edges. Put on a baking sheet. Glaze well with egg then chill for 20 minutes. Glaze again then bake for 20–25 minutes until golden and cooked through. **Serves 2**

Serve these warm with a crisp green salad.

Bean chilli tacos

30 minutes

oil for frying
onion 1 large, chopped
red chilli 1, finely chopped
garlic 2 cloves, finely chopped
mild chilli powder 1 tsp
black-eyed beans 410g can, drained and rinsed
red kidney beans 410g can, drained and rinsed
chopped tomatoes 2 x 400g cans
taco shells 12
coriander leaves a small handful, roughly chopped
lime 1, cut into wedges

■ Heat 1 tbsp oil in a large frying pan and cook the onion and chilli until soft. Add the garlic and chilli powder, and cook for a few more minutes. Add the beans and tomatoes, and simmer for 20 minutes until thick.

■ Heat the taco shells according to the pack instructions. Stir the coriander through the chilli and serve in the tacos with lime wedges alongside. **Serves 4**

Finish the tacos with some grated Cheddar and a dollop of soured cream.

Swede and bacon pies

30 minutes

back bacon rashers 6, trimmed of all fat
olive oil
onion 1, chopped
swede 1 large, peeled and cubed
carrot 1, peeled and sliced
chicken stock 400ml
parsley leaves a small handful, chopped
potatoes 4 large, peeled and halved

You can use the same amount of ingredients to make one big pie, if you like.

■ Put the bacon in a non-stick pan with 1 tbsp olive oil and brown. Remove, and brown the onions in the same oil. Return the bacon to the pan along with the swede and carrot, and season well. Pour in the chicken stock, cover and cook for 5 minutes or until the veg is tender. Stir in the parsley. Divide among 4 individual pie dishes. Keep warm.

■ Meanwhile, cook the potatoes in boiling water until just tender (about 8 minutes). Drain and cool, then mash. Spoon on to the swede mixture, keeping the potato fluffy, and sprinkle with seasoning. Grill until the potato starts to brown. **Serves 4**

Goat's cheese, potato and rosemary pizza

40 minutes

small waxy potatoes 300g, thinly sliced, skin on
olive oil
garlic 1 clove, crushed
rosemary needles from 2 sprigs, chopped
pizza base mix 150g pack
small goat's cheese 150g–200g log, sliced
red onion ½, thinly sliced

■ Heat the oven to 220C/fan 200C/gas 7. Boil the potato slices for 5–6 minutes until just tender, toss with 1 tbsp olive oil and the garlic and rosemary. Make up the pizza base according to the pack instructions and roll out into a rectangle to fit a lightly oiled non-stick baking sheet. Cover with potato slices, leaving a small border. Scatter the goat's cheese and onion over and drizzle with a little more oil. Leave for 10 minutes for the dough to puff up a little then bake for 10–15 minutes until the base is crisp and golden and cooked through. **Serves 2**

Look out for the first young, fresh goat's cheeses in spring. They begin to arrive at cheesemongers and farmers' markets in April.

Sweet potato and broccoli frittata

20 minutes

sweet potato 1, peeled and cut into small cubes
broccoli ½ head, cut into small florets
olive oil
garlic 1 clove, crushed
eggs 2, beaten
soft goat's cheese 50g
salad to serve

■ Cook the sweet potato in boiling water for 8–10 minutes until it is tender, adding the broccoli for the last 5 minutes. Drain well. Heat a little oil in a small, deep frying pan and add the garlic, sweet potato and broccoli. Toss together then spread the vegetables in an even layer in the frying pan and pour on the egg.
■ Cook until the bottom is set then dot with the goat's cheese and grill very briefly until just set. Serve with salad, or in a wholemeal pitta bread with salad.
Serves 2

Butternut squash is also good in place of the sweet potato.

Brussels bubble and squeak with poached egg

20 minutes

onions 2 small, halved and sliced
butter
potatoes 400g, cooked and crushed
Brussels sprouts 200g, cooked and roughly chopped
eggs 4

■ Cook the onions in a knob of butter until really soft. Mix with the potatoes and sprouts, season well, then form into 4 rough, flat cakes. Melt a knob of butter in a non-stick frying pan. Fry the cakes until golden and crusted on both sides. Keep warm in a low oven while you poach the eggs.

■ Bring a wide, shallow pan of water to a simmer, crack in the eggs then turn down the heat and leave for 6–8 minutes until cooked. Drain well, then top each cake with a poached egg and serve.

Serves 4

Brussels sprouts make a great substitute for cabbage in bubble and squeak, and it's a good way of using up cooked leftovers. If starting from scratch, cook the sprouts until just tender with a nice green colour.

Lamb burger pittas

30 minutes

bulghar wheat 4 tbsp
minced lamb 150g
ground cumin 1 tsp
oil
onion 1, cut into thick slices
wholemeal pitta 2 toasted
green salad leaves to serve

■ Cook the bulghar wheat in simmering water for 5 minutes or until tender. Rinse in cold water and drain. Mix with the mince and ground cumin, and season well. Shape into 4 large or 8 small patties.
■ Heat a little oil in a frying pan and cook the patties and onion rounds in a single layer. The lamb will need 4–5 minutes on each side but the onion may cook a little quicker. Stuff the pitta with the lamb burgers and onion. **Serves 2**

Serve these burgers with bought houmous or tzatziki.

Butternut risotto

30 minutes

onion 1 small, chopped
olive oil
thyme leaves from 2 sprigs, chopped
butternut squash or **pumpkin** 250g, peeled and diced
risotto rice 200g
vegetable stock 600ml, hot
parmesan 2 tbsp, freshly grated

■ Fry the onion gently in 1 tbsp oil until soft but not browned. Add the thyme, squash and rice, and stir for a few seconds to coat the grains with oil. Add a couple of ladles of stock and bring to a simmer. Cook, stirring until almost all the stock is absorbed. Add the rest of the stock a little at a time, cooking until each addition is absorbed, until the squash is soft and the rice al dente and creamy. Season well. Divide among 4 bowls and scatter with cheese. **Serves 4**

For extra richness, stir in a large knob of butter right at the end of cooking.

Grilled field mushrooms with rarebit filling

20 minutes

Cheddar cheese 200g
English mustard 1 tsp
egg 1
Worcestershire sauce a dash
cayenne pepper a pinch
field or **portobello mushrooms** 4 large, stalks removed
olive oil
salad leaves to serve

■ Mix the cheese, mustard and egg with a dash of Worcestershire sauce and a pinch of cayenne. Put the mushrooms on a baking sheet, drizzle with olive oil and season. Grill, turning, until just tender. Fill the mushroom cavities with the cheese mix. Grill until golden and bubbling. Serve each mushroom with salad. **Serves 4**

If you can only get smaller mushrooms, cook in the same way and serve 2 or 3 per person.

Huevos rancheros

30 minutes

olive oil
onion 1, finely chopped
red pepper 1, finely chopped
red chilli 1, finely chopped
garlic 1, clove crushed
oregano ½ tsp, dried or fresh
chopped tomatoes 400g can
eggs 2

■ Heat 1 tbsp oil in a large frying pan and add the onion, pepper, chilli, garlic and oregano. Fry gently for about 5 minutes or until everything is soft then add the tomatoes and cook for a further 5 minutes. If the sauce looks dry, add a splash of water. Season well and then make 4 hollows in the mixture, break an egg into each and cover the pan. Cook for 5 minutes or until the eggs are set.
Serves 2

Serve this classic ranch-style Mexican breakfast with warm pitta breads or flour tortillas for scooping.

Mac 'n' cheese pots

1 hour

butter 30g
plain flour 30g
milk 850ml
garlic 1 clove, halved
Dijon mustard 1 tsp
mature Cheddar 200g, grated
Gruyère cheese 100g, grated
Grana Padano or **parmesan** 50g, grated
macaroni 250g

■ Melt the butter in a pan then stir in the flour. Keep cooking and stirring for 3 minutes then gradually whisk in the milk to give a smooth sauce. Add the garlic, simmer for 4 minutes, then fish out. Add the mustard, Cheddar, Gruyère, half the Grana Padano or Parmesan and stir until melted. Season.

■ Heat the oven to 220C/fan 200C/gas 7. Cook the macaroni until just al dente then rinse under cold water and drain well. Mix with the sauce and divide among 4 ovenproof dishes. Scatter over the remaining Grana Padano or Parmesan, then bake for about 15 minutes until golden and bubbling (flash under the grill for a minute if needed). **Serves 4**

For a super-silky finish, whiz the sauce with a hand blender before adding it to the macaroni.

Mini cottage pies

1 hour 20 minutes

olive oil
lean minced beef 500g
onions 2, finely chopped
garlic 2 cloves, crushed
carrots 2 small, finely diced
celery 2 sticks, finely diced
fresh thyme 3 sprigs, leaves stripped
tomato purée 2 tbsp
red wine 250ml
beef stock cubes 2, dissolved in 500ml hot water
parsley 1 small bunch, chopped

HORSERADISH MASH
Maris Piper potatoes 1kg
butter 75g, diced
horseradish cream 2 tbsp
milk 100ml, hot

■ Heat the oven to 200C/fan 180C/gas 6. Heat a large non-stick frying pan with 1 tbsp oil. Fry the mince on a high heat until browned all over. Scoop out then cook the onion, garlic, carrot and celery in the same pan with another tbsp oil until softened. Add back the mince with the thyme and tomato purée, stir well. Turn up the heat and pour in the wine. Bubble until reduced then add the stock and simmer for 30 minutes, covered, until the sauce has reduced and thickened slightly. Stir in the parsley and cool a little.

■ Boil the potatoes until tender. Mash with the butter and horseradish then beat in the milk. Cool a little. Divide the beef mix among 4 individual ovenproof dishes. Spoon over the mash and fluff up the top with a fork. Bake for 20–25 minutes until the peaks are golden and crusted. **Serves 4**

If you don't like horseradish, you could flavour the mash with mustard instead or just leave it plain.

Jansson's temptation

1 hour 10 minutes

butter
potatoes 6 medium, Desirée or Maris Piper, peeled and cut into matchsticks
onions 2 large or 4 small, finely sliced
anchovy fillets 1 can, drained and roughly chopped
double cream 284ml carton
fresh breadcrumbs 4 tbsp
crusty bread, salad or **green veg** to serve

■ Heat the oven to 200C/fan 180C/gas 6. Butter a baking dish measuring about 20 x 30cm and layer in the potatoes, onion and anchovies, starting and finishing with a potato layer. Pour the cream over and dot with a little butter. Sprinkle on the breadcrumbs and a grinding of black pepper – don't add any salt as the anchovies are usually salty enough.

■ Cover and bake for 20 minutes then take the cover off and bake for 25–35 minutes until the top has turned golden brown and the potatoes are soft when tested with the point of a knife. Serve with crusty bread and salad or green veg.

Serves 4

In Sweden, where this dish originates, it would be made with cured sprats rather than anchovies.

Toad-in-the-hole

50 minutes

plain flour 150g
English mustard powder 3 tsp
eggs 2
milk 300ml
thyme 3 sprigs, leaves stripped
pork sausages 8 fat ones
sunflower oil 2 tbsp

■ To make the batter, mix the flour and mustard powder in a bowl with a good pinch of salt. Gradually whisk in the eggs and milk until you have a smooth batter. Mix in the thyme.

■ Heat the oven to 220C/fan 200C/gas 7. Fry the sausages in the oil until golden brown. Put the sausages and any oil in the bottom of an ovenproof dish (you'll need one where you can arrange the sausages evenly with enough space between them for the batter to rise).

■ Put the dish in the oven for 5 minutes to heat. Give the batter another whisk then pour into the hot dish. Put straight back in the oven and cook for 30 minutes until puffed, browned and crisp. **Serves 4**

Adding mustard powder to the batter gives a bit of extra zip to a classic toad.

MAN'S

Italian lamb stew with rosemary and olives

3-3½ hours

boneless lamb shoulder 2.5kg, excess fat trimmed
flour 4 tbsp, well seasoned for dusting
olive oil 3 tbsp
onions 3 large, chopped
celery 4 sticks, diced
carrots 4, peeled and diced
garlic 4 cloves, sliced
rosemary needles 2 tbsp, chopped
white wine 350ml
plum tomatoes 2 x 400g can
black olives 20, pitted
lemons 2, zested and juiced
flat-leaf parsley 1 small bunch, chopped

■ Heat the oven to 160C/fan 140C/gas 3. Cut the lamb into chunks and dust with the flour. Heat 1 tsp of the oil in a large casserole dish. Brown the meat all over in batches and set aside. Pour in the remaining oil, onions, celery, carrots, garlic and rosemary.

■ Season and cook for 10 minutes. Add the wine, tomatoes and meat and bring to a simmer. Cover and cook for 2–3 hours. Stir in the olives and lemon juice, sprinkle with the lemon zest and parsley and serve. **Serves 12**

Lamb shoulder is less expensive than leg, and is meltingly tender when slow-cooked. Serve it on its own or with polenta.

Beef in ale with horseradish dumplings

30 minutes + 2½-3 hours in the oven

oil
braising beef 1kg, cut into large pieces
plain flour 2 tbsp, well seasoned
onions 3, sliced
garlic 1 clove, crushed
button mushrooms 200g
brown ale 500ml
fresh thyme 2 sprigs

HORSERADISH DUMPLINGS
butter 75g, frozen and grated
self-raising flour 150g
horseradish cream or sauce 2 tbsp
thyme 2 sprigs, leaves stripped and chopped

Braising beef is made from the cheaper cuts of meat like chuck and blade, and needs a long, slow braise to get it to tenderness.

■ Heat the oven to 150C/fan 130C/gas 2. Heat a little oil in a large ovenproof casserole. Dust the meat with flour and fry in batches until well browned, then scoop out. Add the onions and fry on a fairly high heat until beginning to soften and brown at the edges, add the garlic for a minute, scoop out. Add the mushrooms and fry until golden. Pour in the ale, let it bubble up, then return the meat, onions and garlic with the thyme. Cover and cook in the oven for 2–2½ hours or until tender.

■ To make the dumplings, mix the butter, flour, horseradish and thyme together and season. Gradually add 1–2 tbsp water to the dry ingredients until you have a firmish dough (you might need a bit more water). Shape into 12 dumplings.

■ To finish the dish, divide the casserole among 4 mini casseroles or heatproof dishes. Put 3 dumplings on top of each and cook, uncovered, for 25 minutes until cooked and golden. **Serves 4**

Caramelized onion tart

1 hour

all-butter shortcrust pastry 500g block
butter 75g
onions 3 large, sliced (about 600g)
double cream 142ml carton
eggs 3
Gruyère 100g, grated

■ Heat the oven to 190C/fan 170C/gas 5. Roll out the pastry to the thickness of a £1 coin and use it to line a rectangular tart tin (approx 34cm x 12cm). Line the pastry with baking paper and fill with blind-baking beans. Bake for 15 minutes, remove the beans and paper, and cook for 10 minutes. Cool.
■ Meanwhile, melt the butter in a large pan. Add the onions and cook over a low heat, stirring occasionally until they are golden and meltingly soft (this will take about 20 minutes so be patient). Whisk together the cream, eggs and cheese, and season well. Stir in the onions then pour into the pastry case. Slide back in the oven for 15–20 minutes until the filling is just set. Serve warm. **Serves 6**

The secret to this tart is cooking the onions slowly until they are really soft and caramelized.

Moussaka

1½ hours

onion 1, finely chopped
olive oil
garlic 1 clove, crushed
minced lamb 750g
ground cinnamon 1 tsp
white wine 100ml
plum tomatoes 400g can
parsley chopped, 2 tbsp
aubergines 2, sliced
milk 600ml
bay leaf 1
black peppercorns 4
butter 75g
flour 75g
potatoes 4 peeled, cooked and sliced
eggs 2

To save time you could use a tub of bought Béchamel sauce and just whisk in the eggs before cooking.

■ Fry the onion in a little oil until soft, then add the garlic. After a minute, add the mince and brown, breaking up any lumps. Add the cinnamon, wine and tomatoes, simmer for 30 minutes, bubble off any excess liquid and stir in the parsley.

■ Meanwhile, brown the aubergines in a little oil on both sides then drain on kitchen paper. Bring the milk to a simmer with the bay leaf and peppercorns. Heat the butter in a pan, stir in the flour and gradually add the milk, stirring continuously until you have a smooth sauce. Strain and season.

■ Heat the oven to 180C/fan 160C/gas 4. Layer the cooked meat sauce and aubergine in an ovenproof dish, top with the potatoes and season. Whisk the eggs into the white sauce and spoon over. Bake for 30–40 minutes until brown.

Serves 6

Feta baked with tomato and oregano

1 hour

olive oil
garlic 2 cloves, sliced
dried chilli flakes a big pinch
plum tomatoes 2 x 400g cans, drained
oregano leaves a small handful, chopped
feta 2 x 200g blocks, broken up into large chunks
crusty bread warmed, to serve

■ Heat 3 tbsp oil in a pan, add the garlic and cook for a minute. Add the chilli and tomatoes, and simmer for 25 minutes until thickened. Season and stir in the oregano.

■ Heat the oven to 200C/fan 180C/gas 6. Put the feta in an ovenproof dish, cover with sauce and bake for 20 minutes before serving. **Serves 4**

Cooked feta keeps its shape but becomes lovely and spreadable. Use the warm crusty bread to scoop up the sauce.

Curly kale and meatball soup

40 minutes

olive oil
onions 2, finely sliced
curly kale 200g, roughly chopped
chicken stock 1 litre
pecorino or **Parmesan,** 4 tbsp, freshly grated

MEATBALLS
white bread 1 slice, soaked in 2 tbsp **milk**
minced pork 250g
salt 1 tsp
egg yolk 1
flat-leaf parsley 2 tbsp, finely chopped
garlic ½ clove, crushed
pecorino or **Parmesan** 2 tbsp, freshly grated

■ Heat 3 tbsp olive oil in a heavy pan. Add the onion, season well and cook until brown and caramelized.

■ Meanwhile, bring a large pan of salted water to the boil. Cook the kale for 4 minutes. Rinse well in cold water and drain.

■ For the meatballs, break up the soaked bread with your fingers. Add the remaining meatball ingredients and mix well. Roll the mixture into marble-sized balls. Fry the meatballs for a few minutes until browned and cooked through. When the onions are ready, add the stock, kale and meatballs and heat through. Ladle into bowls and spoon the cheese over each before serving. **Serves 4**

Curly kale adds a robust texture to soups. You could also use cavolo nero or spring greens.

Chicken and date tagine

1½ hours

chicken thighs 8, on the bone, skin on
butternut squash 1 small, peeled and cut into chunks
red onion 1, cut into wedges
chicken stock 300ml
cherry tomatoes 400g can
cinnamon stick 1
medjool dates 8, halved
coriander leaves 1 large bunch, to garnish
buttered couscous to serve

SPICE PASTE
red onion 1 small, roughly chopped
garlic 2 cloves, roughly chopped
root ginger 3cm piece, roughly chopped
ground cumin 1 tsp
paprika 2 tsp
mild chilli powder 1 tsp
coriander roots 1 large bunch
lemon 1, zested and juiced
olive oil

■ Heat the oven to 190C/fan 170C/gas 5. Put all the spice paste ingredients in a small food processor with 2 tbsp olive oil and whiz to a paste.

■ Brown the chicken thighs all over in a tagine or large, wide pan. Scoop out then add the spice paste and cook for a few minutes until fragrant. Add the squash, onion, stock, tomatoes and cinnamon, and stir. Sit the chicken on top (push down a bit into the sauce).

■ Cook uncovered in the oven for 1 hour – the chicken should be browned and cooked and the sauce reduced. Add the dates for the last 20 minutes of cooking. Scatter with coriander and serve with buttered couscous. **Serves 4**

The dates and squash, both in season now, give this dish a lovely savoury–sweet flavour.

Cauliflower cheese pot pies

45 minutes

crème fraîche 200ml carton
mature Cheddar 100g grated
spring onions 4, shredded
cauliflower 1 head, cut into small florets
frozen peas 100g, defrosted
ready-rolled puff pastry 375g, 4 circles cut out, slightly larger than the pie dishs
egg 1, beaten

■ Heat the oven to 200C/fan 180C/gas 6. Mix the crème fraîche, Cheddar, spring onions, cauliflower and peas, and divide among 4 small ovenproof dishes. Top with the pastry circles, press down firmly and glaze with the egg. Bake for 25–30 minutes until crisp and golden. **Serves 4**

You can use a mix of half cauli, half broccoli, if you prefer more green veg.

Fragrant aubergine curry

40 minutes

groundnut oil
aubergine 3 small, quartered lengthways then halved
coconut milk 400ml
vegetable stock 300ml
ground turmeric 1 tsp
coriander leaves 1 large bunch, roughly chopped
steamed basmati rice to serve

CURRY PASTE
shallots 2, roughly chopped
garlic 2 cloves, roughly chopped
root ginger 1 thumb-sized piece, peeled and roughly chopped
lemon grass 1 stalk, woody outer leaves removed and chopped
green chillies 4, seeded and chopped
coriander stalks from 1 large bunch, roughly chopped
ground cumin 1 tsp
ground coriander 1 tsp

■ Whiz all the curry paste ingredients together in a food processor until you have a rough paste (add water to help).
■ Heat 3 tbsp groundnut oil in a large pan or wok and cook the aubergines until golden. Scoop out.
■ Fry the paste in a little of the coconut milk until fragrant. Add the rest of the coconut milk, stock and turmeric, and bring to a simmer. Add back the aubergine and simmer until it's tender but holding its shape, around 10 minutes. Scatter with coriander leaves and serve with a bowl of steamed basmati rice.
Serves 4

This is an easy way to get a hit of sparky Asian flavours. The secret is not to let the aubergine get too mushy.

Leg of lamb cooked with potatoes

2 hours

leg of lamb 2.5kg
prosciutto or **Parma ham** 6 slices
garlic 4 cloves
lemon 1, zested
fresh rosemary 2 sprigs
butter 25g, softened
Maris Piper potatoes 2kg, peeled and cut into 1cm slices
vegetable stock 500ml

■ Heat the oven to 230C/fan 210C/gas 8. Start by making deep incisions all over the meaty side of the leg of lamb using a small knife.

■ Whiz the Parma ham, garlic, lemon zest and the needles from one rosemary sprig in a food processor. Season with pepper and, using your fingers, push the mixture into the incisions in the lamb. Pull the rest of the rosemary into small sprigs and push into each incision. Spread the butter over the surface of the meat and season well.

■ Season the potatoes, arrange in a roasting tin and pour the stock around. Put the lamb on top and roast for 15 minutes. Turn the heat down to 180C/fan 160C/gas 4 and continue to cook for a further 1 hour and 15 minutes. **Serves 6**

Parma ham or prosciutto will give a lovely, deep savouriness to the lamb.

Roasted butternut squash with goat's cheese

1 hour 20 minutes

butternut squash 2, small
garlic 1 clove, crushed
olive oil 3 tbsp
dried chilli flakes a pinch
fresh thyme 1 tsp, chopped
courgette 1, cut into 2cm chunks
red pepper 1, cut into 2cm chunks
red onions 2 small, cut into thin wedges
cherry tomatoes 200g
pine nuts 50g
breadcrumbs 1 tbsp
parsley 1 tbsp, chopped
Parmesan 1 tbsp
goat's cheese 100g, crumbled

■ Heat the oven to 200C/fan 180C/gas 6. Cut the squash in half and scoop out the seeds then cut criss-cross patterns over the cut-side of each half. Mix together the garlic, 2 tbsp olive oil, chilli and thyme, and brush over the flesh. Bake for 30–40 minutes until tender.

■ To make the filling, put the courgette, pepper and onion in a roasting tin and drizzle with 1 tbsp olive oil. Season and roast for 20–25 minutes until tender. Add the cherry tomatoes and pine nuts, and cook for another 10 minutes.

■ Mix the breadcrumbs, parsley and Parmesan. Arrange the roasted vegetables and goat's cheese in the squash halves, scatter with the breadcrumb mix and bake for a further 10 minutes or until golden and bubbling.

Serves 4

This makes a brilliant main course for vegetarians if everyone else is having a meat roast.

Chicken pot pies

1 hour 15 minutes + chilling

boneless skinless chicken thighs 12
chicken stock 500ml
butter 50g
plain flour 50g
dry white wine 200ml
crème fraîche 200ml
Gruyère 100g, grated
Dijon mustard 1 heaped tsp
tarragon leaves 1 small bunch, chopped
carrots 4 small, chopped and blanched
leeks 2 small, trimmed, sliced and blanched
frozen peas 125g, defrosted
puff pastry 500g block
egg 1, beaten, to glaze

You can use whatever veg you have around to make these pies.

■ Put the chicken in a large, wide pan in a single layer. Pour over the stock, cover and simmer gently for 10 minutes or until cooked through. Strain and reserve the stock, and cut the chicken into chunks.

■ Melt the butter in a pan, add the flour and cook for 30 seconds to make a roux. Add the reserved stock stirring constantly. Add the wine and simmer for 5 minutes then add the crème fraîche and simmer for 5 minutes. Take off the heat, stir in the Gruyère, mustard and tarragon. Season and cool.

■ Divide the chicken and veg among 6 individual ovenproof dishes and pour the sauce over.

■ Heat the oven to 190C/fan 170C/gas 5. Roll out the pastry to the thickness of a £1 coin and cut into circles slightly larger than the pie dishes. Brush the edges of the pie dishes with water, top with pastry and press to seal. Brush with beaten egg, put on a baking sheet and cook for about 35 minutes until the pastry is puffed and golden. **Makes 6**

Roasted tarragon chicken with carrots, leeks and new potatoes

1 hour 30 minutes

butter 50g, softened
garlic 1 clove, crushed
tarragon leaves 1 tbsp, chopped
parsley 1 tbsp, chopped
lemon 1, zested
chicken 1 medium, about 1.5kg
new potatoes 1kg, scrubbed
young carrots 500g
small leeks 500g, trimmed and halved

You can vary the herbs in the butter mix. Try basil, thyme, chives or rosemary instead of tarragon.

■ Heat the oven to 200C/fan 180C/gas 6. Mix the butter, garlic, herbs and lemon zest in a small bowl, and season well. Using your hands, carefully loosen the skin over the chicken breast starting from the neck end. Spread ⅔ of the butter mix between the breast and the skin then smooth the skin back down. Season and roast for 1 hour 15 minutes or until the juices run clear when the thigh is tested with a skewer.

■ Meanwhile, boil the potatoes and carrots in salted water for 5 minutes. Drain well and tip into another roasting tin, add the remaining herby butter and roast above the chicken for 30 minutes or until tender.

■ Cook the leeks for 2 minutes in boiling, salted water, drain well and add to the other veggies. Continue to cook for another 15 minutes. Serve the chicken carved into thick slices with the roasted veggies and the pan juices poured over.

Serves 4

Sea trout and herb fishcakes

45 minutes + chilling

sea trout 500g skinless fillet
potatoes 500g floury ones, such as King Edward or Maris Piper, peeled
spring onions 6, finely shredded
butter
chives and/or **parsley,** a good handful, finely chopped
lemon 2, 1 zested, 1 cut into wedges
egg 1 beaten
fresh breadcrumbs 100g
oil for frying
dressed salad leaves to serve
lemon wedges to serve

Because they head out to sea to feed, wild sea trout or salmon trout often have more flavour than farmed trout, and the firm, pink flesh is perfect for making these fishcakes – but you could use normal trout or salmon, if you like.

■ Heat the oven to 190C/fan 170C/gas 5. Put the fish in a baking dish with a splash of water, cover tightly with foil then bake for 15–20 minutes until just cooked through. Cool and flake into large chunks.

■ Boil the potatoes until tender then mash with lots of seasoning. Cook the spring onions in a little butter until softened then add to the mash with the herbs and lemon zest, and mix in. Gently mix in the trout then leave to cool a little. Form into 8 cakes then dip each first into the beaten egg, then the breadcrumbs. Chill for an hour to set.

■ Heat a little oil in a non-stick frying pan. Cook the fishcakes for 3–4 minutes each side until golden and crisp. Keep warm in a low oven while you finish the rest. Serve with dressed salad leaves and lemon wedges. **Serves 4**

Braised Chinese pork with sesame spring greens

2½ hours, including 2 hours in the oven

garlic 2 cloves, crushed
root ginger 1 thumb-sized piece, grated
soy sauce 2 tbsp
Shaoxing rice wine or **dry sherry** 3 tbsp
star anise 1
Chinese five-spice 1 tsp
cinnamon stick 1
brown sugar 2 tbsp
pork shoulder 1kg, fat trimmed and cut into chunks

SESAME SPRING GREENS
spring greens 500g, washed and stalks removed, shredded
sesame oil
sesame seeds 1 tbsp, toasted

■ Heat the oven to 150C/fan 130C/gas 2. Mix the first 8 ingredients together with 300ml water and put in a large casserole with a lid. Add the pork and stir. Cover and cook for 2 hours. Remove from the oven and scoop out the meat. Fast boil the sauce until reduced and thick enough to coat the pork. Put the pork back in and toss in the sauce to heat through.

■ Meanwhile, heat a large pan or wok and add the greens and a splash of water. Cover and cook until wilted. Dress with sesame oil and seeds, and serve with the pork. **Serves 4**

Don't be put off by the long list of ingredients. This recipe looks lengthy, but it takes care of itself once in the oven.

Roast sirloin with balsamic shallots and Yorkies

1 hour 45 minutes

rolled sirloin of beef 2kg
English mustard powder 1 tsp
shallots 10, peeled
soft brown sugar 1 tbsp
balsamic vinegar 1 tbsp

YORKIES
plain flour 125g
eggs 2
milk 200ml
beef fat or **sunflower oil**

GRAVY
plain flour 1 tbsp
red wine 250ml
beef stock 700ml

Rubbing the beef with mustard powder intensifies the flavour and helps crisp up the fat.

■ Heat the oven to 230C/fan 210C/gas 8. Rub the beef with mustard and season. Cook in a roasting tin for 20 minutes. Add the shallots, turn oven to 160C/fan 140C/gas 3. Cook for 15 minutes per 500g of meat for pink beef. Rest under foil.

■ To make the yorkies, put the flour in a bowl and season. Whisk in the eggs and milk gradually until smooth. Turn the oven to 220C/fan 200C/gas 7. Pour ½tsp beef fat or oil into each hole of a 12-hole muffin tin. Heat in the oven for 5 minutes. Divide the batter among the muffin tins. Cook for 20 minutes until golden and well risen.

■ Meanwhile, put the shallots in a large frying pan, add the sugar and balsamic, and cook, turning, until caramelized.

■ For the gravy, drain all but 1 tbsp fat from the roasting tin. Add the flour and cook over a medium heat for 1 minute stirring constantly. Add the wine and reduce by half. Stir to remove any caramelized bits from the bottom of the pan. Add the stock. Simmer until the gravy has thickened. Serve with the beef.

Serves 6

Fish soup

30 minutes

potatoes 6, peeled and cut into cubes
onion 1, diced
allspice berries 3, lightly crushed (find them in the spice section)
milk 250ml
white fish fillets 750g
North Atlantic peeled prawns 500g
single cream 284ml carton
fresh dill chopped, 2 tbsp

■ Put the potato, onion and allspice in a wide pan with 500ml water, the milk and a pinch of salt. Bring to a boil and simmer for about 15 minutes until the potato is tender. Add the fish, cover, and cook for 3 minutes until opaque, then stir in the prawns, cream and dill, and season. Heat through but don't boil. **Serves 6**

Use a floury potato like King Edward or Maris Piper for this soup. We used small North Atlantic prawns because they have a sweet flavour and are sustainably harvested.

Mushroom and Jarlsberg tart

1¼ hours + chilling

onion 1 medium, finely chopped
butter
mixed mushrooms 750g, sliced if large
shortcrust pastry 500g block (an all-butter version will taste better)
eggs 3, beaten
soured cream 200g
Jarlsberg cheese 2 handfuls, grated

For the filling, try chanterelles or other wild or cultivated mushrooms. If using chanterelles or shiitake mushrooms, take off their woody stems and just use the caps.

■ Fry the onion in a little butter until it is soft but not coloured. Tip on to a plate. Fry the mushrooms on a high heat in a little butter, stirring continually, until all the moisture has evaporated and they are quite dry. Mix in the cooked onion then cool the mixture. Season.

■ Roll out the pastry and use it to line a shallow springform cake tin, about 24cm diameter. The sides of the pastry should be 4–5 cm, high enough to hold the mushroom filling. Chill for 30 minutes and heat the oven to 200C/fan 180C/gas 6. Blind bake the pastry for about 15 minutes, or until it feels firm enough to hold its shape without collapsing, remove the paper and baking beans and cook for 5–10 minutes to dry out the base Fill the base with the mushroom mix.

■ Mix 2/3 of the egg into the soured cream then pour over. Sprinkle the cheese over. Brush the pastry edges with the remaining egg and bake for about 30 minutes, or until the filling has set. Cool a little before removing from the tin.

Serves 8

Herb-stuffed roast pork

2^3/$_4$ hours

pork belly 1.5kg
sage and/or **parsley**, a handful roughly chopped
garlic 2 cloves, crushed
olive oil
leeks 6, trimmed
salt flakes
cider 300ml
sage leaves 4

■ Take the pork belly out of the fridge an hour before you start cooking. Heat the oven to 200C/fan 180C/gas 6. Mix the herbs and garlic with some olive oil and rub over the flesh side. Roll up the pork and secure with butcher's string. Arrange the leeks in a shallow roasting tin. Put the pork on top and rub with salt and pepper. Add the cider and sage.
■ Roast for 20–30 minutes or until the crackling starts to pop, and then turn the oven down to 150C/fan 130C/gas 2 and cook for 2 hours. If the leeks look as though they might be about to burn, add a little water. Rest the meat for 20 minutes before carving. Serve with the leeks and any juices. **Serves 6**

The leeks really benefit from a long, slow cooking time to make them meltingly tender.

Meatballs with mash and lingonberry sauce

40 minutes

minced pork or **veal** 1kg of 1 or a mixture of both
eggs 2
cream 125ml, double or single
fine dry breadcrumbs 60g
onion 1, finely chopped
allspice berries a pinch
whole nutmeg a grating
oil
mashed potatoes to serve
lingonberry sauce to serve

RED WINE SAUCE
plain flour 2 tbsp
beef stock 250ml or use beef consommé
red wine 100ml

■ Mix together the first 7 ingredients and season well. Scoop out tablespoons and roll each into a ball. Heat 2–3 tbsp oil in a frying pan and fry the meatballs in batches for about 10 minutes, shaking the pan to brown them on all sides. Scoop out, drain on kitchen paper and keep warm.

■ To make the red wine sauce, add the flour to the frying pan and stir in, scraping up any bits on the bottom of the pan. Add the stock and red wine, bring to the boil then simmer for a couple of minutes. Taste and add a little water if too strong.

■ Roll the meatballs in the sauce and reheat thoroughly, making sure they are cooked through. Serve with mashed potatoes and lingonberry sauce. **Serves 6**

Lingonberries are a European relation of the cranberry – you can buy lingonberry sauce from Ikea or Scandelicious, or use cranberry sauce instead.

Smoked haddock and leek risotto

45 minutes

smoked haddock 400g
olive oil
butter
leeks 4 young ones, halved lengthways and thinly sliced
carnaroli or **arborio rice** 300g
dry white wine 1 glass
chicken stock 1.5 litres, kept simmering
fresh chives 1 small bunch, snipped

■ Put the haddock in a heatproof dish and just cover with boiling water. Cover with cling film and leave for 10 minutes. Flake into decent-sized chunks.

■ Meanwhile, heat 2 tbsp oil and a knob of butter in a wide, shallow pan then add the leeks. Cook slowly for 10 minutes until completely softened. Turn up the heat, add the rice and stir to coat the grains. Pour in the wine and stir until absorbed. Add the stock, a ladleful at a time, stirring each lot in, until the rice is just tender and creamy (you might not need to use all the stock). Stir in the haddock and chives, and serve. **Serves 4**

Look for pale yellow, natural-coloured smoked haddock rather than the bright yellow, dyed stuff.

Swiss chard, onion and Gruyère tart

45 minutes + 40–50 minutes in the oven

---

all-butter shortcrust pastry 500g block
butter
onions 3 medium, finely sliced
Swiss chard 250g, leaves and stalks separated
eggs 4
double cream 142ml carton
Gruyère 75g, grated
Parmesan 2 tbsp, grated

Swiss chard stems need to be cooked a little longer than the leaves, so separate them before you start. Look for perky green leaves when buying.

■ Heat the oven to 190C/fan 170C/gas 5. Roll out the pastry to the thickness of a £1 coin and line a 23cm, loose-bottomed tart tin. Line with a circle of baking paper and fill with baking beans. Cook for 10 minutes then take out the beans and paper and cook for another 10 minutes. Turn the oven down to 180C/fan 160C/gas 4.

■ Heat a knob of butter in a pan and cook the onions until completely softened. Add the Swiss chard stalks first and cook for 3 minutes then add the leaves, and keep cooking until tender. Season and cool.

■ Mix together the eggs, cream and cheeses, and season well. Spread the chard and onion over the base of the tart and pour the egg mix over. Cook for 20–30 minutes until the filling is just set.

Serves 4–6

Garlicky potato and mushroom gratin

1 hour

waxy potatoes (such as Charlotte) 450g, peeled
portobello mushrooms 150g, thickly sliced
olive oil for frying
bay leaf 1
double cream 200ml
milk 100ml
Dijon mustard 1 tsp
smoked garlic cloves 2, chopped
flat-leaf parsley 1 small bunch, roughly chopped
Gruyère cheese 50g, grated

■ Heat the oven to 180C/fan 160C/gas 4. Simmer the potatoes in boiling, salted water for 5 minutes, drain and slice. Meanwhile, fry the mushrooms in a little olive oil with the bay leaf until golden and all the moisture has bubbled off. Layer the potatoes in a buttered baking dish with the mushrooms.

■ Mix the cream, milk, mustard, garlic and parsley together and season. Pour over the potatoes and mushrooms, sprinkle the Gruyère over, and bake for 30–40 minutes, until the potatoes are tender and the top is golden. **Serves 2**

Most large supermarkets sell smoked garlic, but you can just substitute 1 clove of regular garlic, if you like.

Toulouse sausage and butter bean casserole

40 minutes

Toulouse sausages 6
oil
rindless streaky bacon rashers 6, chopped
leek 1 large, sliced
garlic 1 clove, sliced
white wine 1 large glass
chicken stock 200ml
dried chilli flakes a pinch
butter beans 2 x 400g cans, drained and rinsed
parsley 1 small bunch, roughly chopped

■ Brown the sausages in a little oil then scoop out and slice into chunks. Brown the bacon in the same pan then add the leeks and garlic, and cook till softened. Add back the sausages, the wine, stock, chilli flakes and the beans. Simmer for 10–15 minutes until the sausages are cooked through. Season and add the parsley. **Serves 4**

Toulouse sausages have a lovely spicy flavour, but any sausage with a good amount of herbs or garlic would work.

Sugar-crust cherry pie

1 hour 30 mins

cherries 500g, stoned
caster sugar 2–3 tbsp
kirsch 1 tbsp
demerara sugar 2 tbsp
vanilla ice cream to serve

SWEET PASTRY
plain flour 400g
butter 200g, cold, diced
caster sugar 50g
egg yolks 2, plus 1 for glazing

Soaking the fruit first in kirsch really bumps up the cherry flavour of this pie.

■ Toss the cherries and sugar together with the kirsch, and leave to macerate for 20 minutes.

■ To make the pastry, put the flour in a food processor, add the butter and pulse to breadcrumbs. Add the caster sugar and mix. Add the 2 egg yolks and pulse until the mixture comes together (you might need to add a splash of cold water as well). Wrap in cling film and chill for 20 minutes.

■ Heat the oven to 190C/fan 170C/gas 5. Roll out half the pastry and line 1 large or 4 small pie dishes. Put the cherry mixture in the bottoms then roll out the rest of the pastry and drape over the tops and trim. Crimp and seal the edges then glaze all over with the remaining egg yolk. Bake for 30–35 minutes until the pastry is crisp and golden. In the last 5 minutes of cooking, sprinkle the demerara sugar over. Rest for 10 minutes before serving with vanilla ice cream. **Serves 4**

Easiest-ever chocolate fudge cake

45 minutes

butter 175g, softened
self-raising flour 150g
cocoa powder 30g
baking powder 1 tsp
light muscovado sugar 175g
eggs 3
vanilla extract 1 tsp
plain chocolate 50g, melted

FUDGE ICING
butter 200g, softened
icing sugar 200g
plain chocolate 200g, melted

■ Heat the oven to 180C/fan 160C/gas 4. Line and butter 2 x 20cm sandwich tins. Put all cake ingredients into the food processor and whiz until smooth. if the mix is a little stiff, add 1–2 tbsp water and whiz again. Divide between tins, level and bake for 30 minutes or until springy. Leave for 5 minutes then cool on a wire rack. Clean the food processor. Whiz the butter and icing sugar, add the chocolate, whiz again, then sandwich and ice the cake. **Serves 10**

Make sure all your ingredients are at room temperature so the mixtures combine properly.

Lemon self-saucing pudding

1 hour

butter 50g
caster sugar 200g
lemon 1, zested
lemon juice 100ml (include the juice from the zested lemon)
eggs 3, separated
plain flour 50g, sifted
milk 250ml
icing sugar for dusting

■ Heat the oven to 180C/fan 160/gas 4. Whiz the butter, sugar and lemon zest together in a food processor. Add the lemon juice, egg yolks, flour and milk one by one until you have a smooth batter. Whisk the egg whites until firm but not stiff, and fold the 2 mixtures together.
■ Pour into a buttered ovenproof soufflé or baking dish and put it in a high-sided baking sheet half filled with hot water. Bake for 45–50 minutes until the top is lightly browned and set and there is a sort of gooey lemon curd below. Remove the dish from the tray, dust with icing sugar and serve. **Serves 4**

Serve this pudding hot with cream or custard, or just on its own.

Steamed syrup pudding

2 hours 15 minutes

soft brown sugar 150g
butter 150g softened, plus extra for buttering the dish
lemon 1, zested
eggs 3, beaten
self-raising flour 150g, mixed with a pinch of salt
golden syrup 8 tbsp
cream or **custard** to serve

It's worth seeking out a plastic pudding basin with a lid. It makes it much easier to turn out your puddings, and you just have to clip on the lid for cooking.

■ Butter a 1.1 litre pudding dish. Put the sugar and butter in a large bowl and beat with electric beaters until pale and fluffy. Beat in the lemon zest and eggs (add a couple of tbsp of flour to help) then fold in the flour. Mix in 3 tbsp syrup. Put another 3 tbsp of the syrup in the bottom of the pudding dish. Spoon the sponge mix on top.

■ Clip on the lid or cover the basin with a pleated sheet of baking parchment and foil. Secure with string and cut off any excess paper/foil.

■ Put the basin in a steamer or in a large pan on an upturned saucer (to stop it touching the base of the pan) with simmering water coming a third of the way up the sides of the dish. Steam for 2 hours, checking the water now and again, and topping up if needed.

■ Rest the pud for a couple of minutes before turning out (if you need to, use a palette knife to loosen). Heat the last 2 tbsp of syrup and pour over to finish. Serve with lots of cream or custard.

Serves 6

LYLE'S GOLDEN
ABRAM LYLE & SONS

Brioche French toast with warm blueberry compote

30 minutes

eggs 2
milk 4 tbsp
caster sugar 1 tbsp
vanilla extract a drop
brioche 4 thick slices, from a loaf
butter for frying
vanilla ice cream to serve

BLUEBERRY COMPOTE
blueberries 100g
caster sugar 1 tbsp
lemon a squeeze of juice

■ Put the compote ingredients in a pan. Heat gently until the blueberries start to pop and release their juice then simmer for 2–3 minutes until jammy.

■ To make the French toast, mix together the eggs, milk, sugar and vanilla extract until the sugar has dissolved. Dip the brioche in the egg mix so it is thoroughly coated. Fry slices in the butter until golden brown on both sides. Serve the French toast with a scoop of vanilla ice cream and the blueberry compote.

Serves 2

Use vanilla extract, which is a natural flavouring, rather than vanilla essence, which is an artificial one.

Cinnamon doughnuts

45 minutes + rising time

active dry yeast 1 pack (1 tbsp)
plain flour 500g, plus more for dusting
caster sugar 100g, plus more for coating
natural yoghurt 1 tbsp
eggs 3 yolks
butter 25g, melted and cooled
groundnut oil or **rapeseed oil** for deep-frying
ground cinnamon for dusting

CHOCOLATE SAUCE
plain chocolate 200g, broken into chunks
double cream 142ml carton

You can buy good bought chocolate or toffee sauce for this, if you want to speed things up.

■ Mix the yeast with 135ml warm water. Stand for 5 minutes, until foamy. Add 125g of the flour. Mix until combined, cover and leave until doubled in size. Add the remaining flour, the sugar, yoghurt and a pinch of salt, then add the egg yolks and cooled melted butter. Beat until the dough comes together (2 minutes). Knead for a minute then put in an oiled bowl and cover. Leave to rise until doubled in size.

■ Cut the dough in half, cover with cling film. Roll out each piece on a floured surface to 1cm thick. Using a very small round cutter (3cm max), cut out rounds. Put on a piece of baking parchment and leave for 15 minutes.

■ Make the chocolate sauce by melting the chocolate and cream in a pan.

■ Heat a pan or a deep fryer ⅓ full of oil until it's hot enough to brown a cube of bread in 1 minute. Fry the doughnuts in batches (about 1 minute each side until golden brown). Drain on kitchen paper. Mix the sugar and a little cinnamon and roll the doughnuts in it. Serve warm with the chocolate sauce. **Makes 24**

Upside-down banana pudding

1 hour

sultanas 100g
rum 50ml
bananas 4 large or 6 small
golden syrup 6 tbsp
butter 75g, softened
caster sugar 100g
egg 1
vanilla extract 1 tsp
self-raising flour 175g
pecan nuts 60g
crème fraîche or **cream** to serve

Use ripe (but not too ripe) bananas for this as you want them to keep their shape.

■ Soak the sultanas in the rum for 30 minutes. Heat the oven to 160C/fan 140C/gas 3. Line the base of a 23cm x 13cm loaf tin with baking parchment. Cut 2 of the bananas into sections that fit the width of the tin, then halve lengthways. Pour the golden syrup along the base of the tin and cover with the banana pieces, cut-side down, fitting them in to make a neat, even layer.

■ Whiz the butter and sugar in a food processor, add the egg, remaining bananas and vanilla extract, and whiz again. Tip into a bowl and fold in the flour, pecans and sultanas. Spoon on to the bananas, being careful not to move them, level the top and bake for 45 minutes or until cooked through (test with a skewer, but don't push it in all the way or you'll hit the banana).

■ Leave for 10 minutes so the syrup soaks into the cake, then turn out on to a plate and serve with crème fraîche or cream. **Serves 6**

Toffee apple and Calvados pancakes

30 minutes

butter
demerara sugar 1 tbsp
apples 3 peeled, cored and cut into wedges
Calvados 3 tbsp
ready-made crêpes 4, available from larger supermarkets
thick cream or **vanilla ice cream** to serve
dulce de leche (or other toffee sauce) warmed, to serve

■ Melt a knob of butter with the sugar in a frying pan. Add the apple wedges and cook until golden and tender. Add the Calvados and either flambé or bubble away for 2–3 minutes. Warm the crêpes, divide the apple mix among them and fold in quarters. Serve 1 or 2 crêpes per person (depending on size) with a dollop of cream and a drizzle of toffee sauce. **Serves 4**

Calvados goes well with the apples, but dark rum or brandy would also work well.

Coffee and walnut cake

1 hour

butter 125g, at room temperature
caster sugar 125g
eggs 2
self-raising flour 125g
baking powder 1 tsp
instant coffee powder 2 heaped tbsp, dissolved in 100ml water
walnut halves 100g

ICING
butter 200g
icing sugar 200–300g

It's always worth toasting nuts in a dry frying pan before using them in cooking as it really brings out their flavour.

■ Heat the oven to 160C/fan 140C/gas 3. Line a deep 18cm loose-bottomed or springform cake tin. Beat the butter and sugar together with electric beaters and then beat in the eggs, flour and baking powder. Beat in 1 tbsp of the coffee mixture and then add up to another tbsp little by little until the mixture drops easily off the spoon. Keep the rest of the coffee mixture for the icing.

■ Stir in half the walnuts, snapping them in half first. Spoon into the tin, level the top and bake for 40 minutes or until a skewer comes out cleanly. Cool.

■ To make the icing, beat the butter until soft and then beat in 200g icing sugar followed by the rest of the coffee mixture until you have a depth of colour and flavour that you like. If the icing looks a little soft, beat in extra icing sugar.

■ Cut the cake into 3 slices horizontally and then sandwich the layers together with some of the icing, you need a reasonably thick layer. Ice the top of the cake with the rest of the icing and decorate with the rest of the walnuts.

Serves 8

Fluffy coconut and lime cake

1 hour + cooling

caster sugar 200g
butter 200g, softened
eggs 4, beaten
self-raising flour 200g
baking powder 1 tsp
lime 1, zested and juiced
creamed coconut ½ x 200g block, grated
sweetened coconut flakes to decorate

FROSTING
eggs 2, whites only
granulated sugar 200g
vanilla extract ½ tsp

■ Heat the oven to 190C/fan 170C/gas 5. Line 2 x 20cm sandwich tins. Beat the sugar, butter, eggs, flour, baking powder, lime zest and juice and creamed coconut together. Divide between the cake tins, level off the surface and bake for 20 minutes or until risen and golden. Cool completely.

■ To make the frosting, whisk the egg whites to stiff peaks. Combine the sugar with 4 tbsp water and boil until you have a thick, clear syrup. Beat the syrup into the egg whites, adding it in a thin stream, and stir in the vanilla. Sandwich the cake together with frosting then frost the outside. Gently press flakes of coconut all over the outside. **Serves 10**

Look for natural coconut flakes in health food shops – they have a much better flavour than desiccated coconut.

Plum and almond crumbles

35 minutes

red plums 6 really ripe, halved, stoned and quartered
demerara sugar 4 tbsp
fresh orange juice 100ml
ground cinnamon 1 tsp

CRUMBLE TOPPING
plain flour 150g
butter 75g
demerara sugar 2 tbsp
rolled oats 4 tbsp
flaked almonds 50g

■ Heat the oven to 180C/fan 160C/gas 4. Put the plums, sugar, orange juice and cinnamon in a pan. Stir and heat for 3–4 minutes until the sugar has dissolved. Divide among 4 small ovenproof dishes. Whiz the flour and butter in a food processor until it resembles breadcrumbs then mix in the sugar, oats and almonds. Spoon over the top of the plums and bake for 20–25 minutes until golden and crisp. **Serves 4**

You'll need really ripe plums for this so they give up their juices – woolly ones just won't work – which is why it's best to wait until they are in season in the autumn.

Blueberry crumble cakes

1 hour

pecan nuts 30g
unsalted butter 125g, very soft
golden caster sugar 125g
eggs 2
self-raising flour 125g
ground cinnamon ½ tsp
blueberries 100g
milk 1 tbsp

CRUMBLE TOPPING
unsalted butter 15g
self-raising flour 50g
pecan nuts 40g, roughly chopped
light muscovado sugar 30g
ground cinnamon ¾ tsp

You can also make these in individual muffin tins. Just line the bottoms with circles of parchment and divide the mixes among the holes.

■ Heat the oven to 180C/fan 160C/gas 4. To make the crumble, rub the butter into the flour until it resembles breadcrumbs and stir in the nuts, sugar and cinnamon. Chill.

■ Line a 20 x 20cm-square cake tin with non-stick baking parchment.

■ Blitz the pecans in a mini food processor until coarsely ground. Beat the butter and sugar together until pale and fluffy, gradually beat in the eggs and sift the flour, cinnamon and a pinch of salt over. Fold the spiced flour in with the ground pecans, blueberries and milk. The mixture will be quite thick but this prevents the blueberries from sinking as the cakes rise. Pour into the cake tin or divide evenly among the paper cases.

■ Sprinkle with the topping mixture and bake for 25–30 minutes, until risen and golden. A fine skewer inserted into a cake should come out dry with no uncooked batter stuck to it. Cool on a wire rack. Cut the cake into squares. **Makes 9**

White chocolate and Baileys cheesecake

1 hour 50 minutes + chilling

chocolate biscuits 175g
unsalted butter 60g, melted
white chocolate 150g, chopped
soft cheese 600g
crème fraîche 300g
caster sugar 200g
vanilla pod 1, split open for seeds
eggs 3 large, at room temperature
Baileys Irish Cream 60ml

Make sure your melted chocolate has cooled before adding to the cheese mix, otherwise it might seize.

■ Heat the oven to 180C/fan 160C/gas 4. Base line a 23cm springform cake tin with baking parchment. Whiz the biscuits to crumbs in a food processor, trickle the melted butter in and whiz again. Spread over the base of the tin and press down. Bake for 10 minutes then cool.

■ Melt half the chocolate in a bowl set over simmering water or in the microwave. Cool. Using a food processor or electric whisk, beat the soft cheese until smooth, then beat in the crème fraîche, sugar and vanilla seeds. Beat in the eggs bit by bit until you have a glossy mixture. Fold in the melted chocolate and the rest of the chopped chocolate and stir in the Baileys. Pile everything into the tin and smooth.

■ Put a tin of water on the base of the oven to create steam. Put the cheesecake on the middle shelf. Cook for 50 minutes–1 hour – the cake should wobble a little when moved but look puffy and set. Turn the oven off, open the door a little. Leave the cake to cool completely. Chill for at least 4 hours. Decorate with chocolate shavings. **Serves 8-10**

Rhubarb, cinnamon and brown sugar muffins

45 minutes

rhubarb 300g, chopped
golden caster sugar 3 tbsp + 100g
milk 200ml
eggs 2, beaten
butter 100g, melted and cooled
plain flour 300g
baking powder 1 tsp
ground cinnamon 1 tsp
demerara sugar to decorate

■ Heat the oven to 200C/fan 180C/gas 6 and line a 12-hole muffin tin with paper cases. Mix the rhubarb with the 3 tbsp sugar and bake for about 10 minutes until just tender. Drain really well and cool on kitchen paper.

■ Whisk together the milk, eggs and butter. Put the flour, baking powder, 100g of sugar and cinnamon in a bowl. Stir the wet ingredients into the dry ones along with the rhubarb. Divide among the muffin cases, sprinkle the tops with demerara sugar and bake for 25–30 minutes until risen and golden. **Makes 12**

Don't overmix the muffin ingredients – you get a lighter result if the mix is a bit lumpy.

Gooseberry, elderflower and vanilla fools

30 minutes

gooseberries 300g, topped and tailed
caster sugar 2 tbsp
elderflower cordial 3 tbsp
double cream 284ml carton
vanilla extract ½tsp
fresh vanilla custard 250ml, available in cartons from the supermarket chiller cabinet

■ Put the gooseberries in a pan with the sugar and 2 tbsp water. Gently stew until the gooseberries are soft and pulpy. Mix in the elderflower cordial and leave to cool.

■ Softly whip the cream with the vanilla extract. Mix the gooseberry pulp with the custard. Take 6 glasses and fill with alternative layers of cream and gooseberry custard. Decorate with whole poached gooseberries, if you like. **Serves 6**

Gooseberries are often paired with elderflower as they come into season at the same time in July, and they really compliment each other.

Black Forest knickerbockers

20 minutes + chilling

pitted black cherries in syrup 425g can, drained
kirsch 1 tbsp (optional)
double chocolate muffin 1, sliced
vanilla ice cream 2 small scoops
cherry or **chocolate ice cream** 2 small scoops
double cream 100ml, lightly whipped with 1 tbsp **icing sugar**
grated chocolate and **chopped toasted whole almonds** to serve

CHOCOLATE SAUCE
golden syrup 2 tbsp
plain chocolate 100g, broken into pieces

■ To make the chocolate sauce, bring 80ml water to the boil with the golden syrup. Remove from the heat and add the broken chocolate, stirring until the sauce is smooth.
■ Toss the cherries with the kirsch, if using, and put a few in the base of each serving glass. Top with a slice of muffin, a scoop of each ice cream and some chocolate sauce. Repeat the layers, finishing with a spoonful of cream, a cherry and a drizzle of sauce. Sprinkle with grated chocolate and chopped almonds. **Serves 2**

Knickerbocker glories were made for a free-style approach – use fresh fruit in the summer and vary the sauce, cake and ice cream, as you fancy.

Sherry trifle

30 minutes + chilling

raspberry jam 4 tbsp
Madeira or **lemon cake** 300g, thickly sliced and halved
raspberries 300g, defrosted frozen ones are fine, plus extra for decoration
sweet sherry 4–6 tbsp
custard powder 2 tbsp
caster sugar 1 tbsp
milk 500ml
double cream 284ml carton + 142ml carton
flaked almonds a handful, toasted

■ Spread a little jam on each slice of cake. Arrange on the bottom of a glass dish. Spoon over the raspberries and squish down a little with a fork then sprinkle over the sherry. Put the custard powder and sugar into a bowl and mix in 2 tbsp of the milk. Heat the rest of the milk then gradually pour over the powder, mixing all the time. Return to the pan and simmer for a few minutes until thickened.

■ Leave custard to cool to room temperature then spoon over the raspberries. Chill for 30 minutes. Softly whip the cream and dollop over the custard. Scatter over the almonds and raspberries then chill for an hour before serving. **Serves 6**

You can use good bought custard if you want to cheat this step of the recipe.

BIRD
CUST
IRDS
USTA

Sticky toffee pudding

50 minutes

medjool dates 180g, stoned and diced
unsalted butter 50g, softened
caster sugar 100g
soft dark brown sugar 75g
eggs 2
self-raising flour 175g

TOFFEE SAUCE
double cream 300ml
demerara sugar 50g
black treacle 2 tsp

■ Heat the oven to 180C/fan 160C/gas 4 and butter 4 x 200ml ovenproof pudding basins. Simmer the dates in 300ml water for 5 minutes until softened. Leave to cool. Cream together the butter and sugars. Add the eggs. Mix in the dates, date liquid and flour. Pour into the pudding basins and bake for 25–30 minutes until just firm. Leave to cool for a couple of minutes before turning out.
■ To make the toffee sauce, put the cream, sugar and treacle in a pan. Heat gently until the sugar has dissolved, then boil for 2–3 minutes, stirring until you have a smooth sauce. Serve with the pudding. **Serves 4**

You can use any dates for this, but medjool are best as they have a natural toffee flavour.

Fallen chocolate truffle cake with Amaretto cream

1 hour

70 per cent plain chocolate 250g, broken into pieces
butter 150g, cubed, plus extra for the tin
golden caster sugar 150g
eggs 5, separated
ground almonds 30g
Amaretto or **bourbon** 1 tbsp
cocoa powder for dusting

AMARETTO CREAM
double cream 142ml carton
icing sugar 2 tbsp
Amaretto or **bourbon** 1 tbsp

You can make this a day ahead – the texture gets even more velvety overnight.

■ Heat the oven to 160C/fan 140C/gas 3. Butter and line the base of a 23cm-round springform cake tin. Melt the chocolate and butter together either in the microwave or in a heatproof bowl set over a pan of simmering water. Stir until smooth. Allow to cool a little, then add 50g sugar and 1 egg yolk. Gradually add remaining egg yolks as you mix. Stir in the almonds and Amaretto.

■ Whisk the egg whites with a pinch of salt until they hold soft peaks then gradually whisk in the remaining sugar, 2 tbsp at a time until the meringue is stiff and glossy. Loosen the chocolate mixture with a spoonful of egg white then fold in the rest of the meringue, trying to retain as much of the volume as possible. Pour into the tin and bake for 30–35 minutes.

■ Leave to cool in the tin on a wire rack for 15 minutes. It will sink but don't worry. Remove from the tin to cool.

■ To make the Amaretto cream, whip the cream, sugar and Amaretto until it just holds its shape. Dust the cake with cocoa and serve with the Amaretto cream.

Serves 8

Mini lemon curd sponge puddings

20 minutes

butter 100g, plus extra for the moulds
caster sugar 100g
lemons 2, zested and juiced
eggs 2
self-raising flour 100g
lemon curd 6 tbsp

■ Butter 4 x 150ml plastic pudding moulds. Whiz the butter, sugar and lemon zest in a food processor until pale and fluffy. Mix in the eggs one by one. Add the flour and pulse until incorporated. Divide among the moulds then cover with a lid or cling film and microwave on Medium (650W) for 4 minutes.

■ Heat the lemon curd with a squeeze of lemon juice in a small pan. Spoon over the top and serve. **Serves 4**

Use lime or orange curd for a variation of this pud.

Apple steamed pudding with a sticky toffee sauce

40 minutes + 1½ hours steaming

unsalted butter 175g, softened
eating apples 4, peeled, cored and cut into 2cm chunks
golden caster sugar 130g
walnuts pieces 50g, toasted and roughly chopped
eggs 3, beaten
self-raising flour 150g

TOFFEE SAUCE
light muscovado sugar 175g
unsalted butter 125g
crème fraîche 200g

You need eating apples rather than Bramleys for this as they will keep their shape during cooking.

■ Melt 25g butter in a large pan, add the apple and cook until just tender then add 1 tbsp sugar and cook for a couple of minutes until the apples start to caramelize. Cool and add the walnuts.

■ To make the sauce, tip all of the ingredients into a pan and cook until melted. Simmer for 2 minutes.

■ Tip the apple and walnut mixture into a buttered 1.5 litre pudding basin. Pour ⅓ of the toffee sauce over. Beat the remaining butter and caster sugar until pale and creamy. Gradually beat in the eggs. Fold in the flour with a pinch of salt. Spoon the mixture on top of the apples and spread level. Cover with a pleated sheet of baking parchment and foil, tie with string, trimming any excess.

■ Sit the bowl on an upturned saucer in a large pan and pour boiling water around the bowl so that it comes halfway up the sides. Cover with a lid. Steam for 1 ½ hours. Add more water to the pan halfway though if needed. Rest the pudding for 2 minutes before turning out on to a dish and serving with the remaining warm toffee sauce. **Serves 8**

Bakewell tart

1 hour 30 minutes + chilling

sweet dessert pastry 500g block
egg white 1, for brushing

FILLING
raspberry jam 2 heaped tbsp
unsalted butter 150g, at room temperature
caster sugar 150g
eggs 3, beaten
egg yolk 1
ground almonds 150g
lemon 1, zested
flaked almonds 1 tbsp
icing sugar for dusting
cream or **custard** to serve

Chilling the pastry before baking means there is less chance of it shrinking in the oven.

■ Roll out the pastry to about 3mm thickness. Line a 20cm x 3 ½cm tart tin. Prick the base with a fork and chill for 20 minutes. Heat the oven to 180C/fan 160C/gas 4. Line the pastry case with baking parchment and fill with baking beans. Cook for about 20 minutes until the pastry is pale gold. Take out the beans, brush the inside of the pastry case with egg white and cook for 2 minutes. Cool slightly.

■ Spread the jam in an even layer over the base of the pastry case. Cream together the butter and caster sugar, add the beaten eggs and egg yolk. Fold in the ground almonds and lemon zest. Spoon the mixture over the jam and spread level. Bake for 20 minutes. Scatter with the flaked almonds and continue to cook for a further 15–20 minutes until golden. Cool to room temperature, dust with icing sugar and serve with cream or custard. **Serves 8**

Lemon polenta cake with limoncello syrup

1 hour 15 minutes

butter 250g, softened
caster sugar 250g
eggs 3
polenta 100g
ground almonds 250g
baking powder 1 tsp
lemons 3 (3 zested, 1 juiced)
limoncello syrup made by warming 4 tbsp **limoncello liqueur** with 3 tbsp **icing sugar**

■ Heat the oven to 160C/fan 140C/gas 3. Butter and base line a 23cm springform tin. Beat together the butter and sugar until light and fluffy (use an electric hand whisk). Add the eggs one by one and beat between each addition. Fold in the polenta, almonds and baking powder. Mix in the lemon zest and juice.

■ Bake for 50 minutes–1 hour until the cake is risen and golden (cover the top of the cake loosely with foil after 30 minutes to stop it browning too much). Serve slices warm with a drizzle of limoncello syrup. **Serves 8**

Using polenta and ground almonds gives this cake a lovely moist texture and also makes it suitable for people who can't have flour in their diet.

Index

Picture credits and recipe credits

BBC Books and **olive** magazine would like to thank the following for providing photographs. While every effort has been made to trace and acknowledge all photographers, we would like to apologize should there be any errors or omissions.

Peter Cassidy p107; Jean Cazals p51–p57, p99, p103, p109, p121, p123, p175, p177; Gus Filgate p63, p75, p111–117, p127, p141, p151, p153, p157, p173, p189, p191, p197, p199, p203; Gareth Morgans p69, p169, p205; David Munns p45, p119, p133, p165, p193; Myles New p183, p211; Michael Paul p47, p49, p83, p89, p105, p145, p147, p164; Brett Stevens p77, p187; Simon Walton p11–25, p29, p31, p35, p41, p59, p61, p65, p71, p73, p93, p185; Philip Webb p33, p43, p79, p81, p85, p87, p91, p95, p97, p101, p125, p129, p131, p135, p137, p139, p143, p149, p155, p159, p161, p167, p171, p179, p181, p195, p201, p207, p209; Simon Wheeler p39; Kate Whittaker p27, p37, p67

All the recipes in this book have been created by the editorial team at **olive** magazine.

Thanks to Paul Merrett for granting permission to use his recipe for *Sticky toffee pudding* p200